That Illustrious Island...
IONA
THROUGH TRAVELLERS' EYES

That Illustrious Island...
IONA
THROUGH TRAVELLERS' EYES

Edited by
MAIRI MACARTHUR

THE NEW IONA PRESS

Published by The New Iona Press Ltd, Old Printing Press Building, Isle of Iona, Argyll PA76 6SL.

ISBN 0 9516283 1 3

Typeset by Nevisprint Ltd, Fort William.
Printed and bound in Great Britain by
Highland Printers Ltd, Inverness.

Cover plate: passengers disembarking at Iona from paddle-steamer *The Grenadier,* September 1909. Photo taken by visitor Miss McFee.

Nineteenth century engraving by W. Banks shows visitors admiring the Cathedral ruins while local people gather in the harvest.

ACKNOWLEDGEMENTS

The New Iona Press is grateful to the following for permission to copy or reproduce photographs : Mrs. Joan Faithfull, Dalkeith (Plates 8, 14); Angus Johnston, Iona (Plate 12); Dugald MacArthur, Connel (Plates 1, 6); Mrs. Dinah MacCormick, Glenrothes (Plate 10); Mrs. Jane MacFadyen, Iona (Plate 16); Maxwell MacLeod, Edinburgh (Plates 4, 5,11, from glass slides thought to be part of a collection made by architect MacGregor Chalmers); National Maritime Museum, Greenwich (cover, Plate 13); Scottish Ethnological Archive, National Museums of Scotland (Plate 9); Harold Troup, Iona (Plate 3).
Thanks also to Roy Pederson for assistance with design and graphics.

CONTENTS

Saloon **Steamer**

INTRODUCTION

> We were now treading that illustrious Island, which was once the luminary of the Caledonian regions, whence savage clans and roving barbarians derived the benefits of knowledge, and the blessings of religion. To abstract the mind from all local emotion would be impossible, if it were endeavoured, and would be foolish if it were possible. ...That man is little to be envied whose patriotism would not gain force upon the plain of Marathon, or whose piety would not grow warmer among the ruins of Iona.

These words of Dr. Samuel Johnson, spoken on his arrival in Iona in 1773 and recorded by his companion James Boswell, are among the best known ever written about the island. Later travellers often quoted this passage in their own accounts. Dr. Johnson's description of his Hebridean journey, published in 1775, became a bestseller and inspired many to follow in his steps.

People have made their way to this tiny island off the western tip of Mull for at least fourteen hundred years. The monastery founded there by Columba in 563 AD drew a steady stream of visitors and pilgrims over succeeding centuries. Tradition holds that Kenneth, first King of the Picts and Scots, and many who reigned after him, were taken to Iona for burial. It became a place of great historical and spiritual importance throughout Scotland and beyond.

Many of these travellers wrote down, sketched, painted or photographed their impressions of Iona - its ruins and crosses, its houses and landscape, its rocks and birdlife, the changing colours of its sea and sky. This book brings together a small selection from the thousands of words and pictures which the island has inspired. The extracts have been chosen primarily for the light that they shed on the people who have lived there and on their way of life.

Travellers' accounts cannot, of course, tell the whole story. Before hotel accommodation and houses to let became available in the late 19th century, few stayed more than two or three hours. Fewer still were able to converse directly with the inhabitants who, with the exception of the schoolmaster, had little or no English up until the early 19th century. And very few indeed will have considered doing so anyway. The prime object of their journey was to see Iona's famous ruins, laden with sacred and historic associations. For many, therefore, the local population represented little more than a passing curiosity and the comments of some visitors are patronising and even insulting. But the observations of others reflect genuine interest, respect and affection. What they recorded often corroborates information from documentary and oral sources. Occasionally they provide unique evidence.

This collection of extracts does not pretend to be a guide to the island today, with its modern lifestyle and amenities. Yet much of what has endured into the late twentieth century - working the land and sea, servicing the tourists, the links of kinship and community - has deep roots in the life that is now past. These accounts are simply one lens through which we can gain glimpses of that past.

How did the islanders, on the other hand, view the travellers? That, regrettably but inevitably, has gone unreported. There is no evidence, however, that visitors were unwelcome. From several of the passages we can see that the people took advantage, naturally enough, of the chance to earn extra cash through the sale of mementoes to the steamship passengers or of milk, butter and potatoes to those who came by yacht. The rule of offering hospitality, to strangers as to their own kin, was clearly strong. And local people took a pride in acting as guides to the historic ruins.

Islander and traveller belonged, of course, to very different worlds. Dr. Sacheverell, crossing Mull on his way to Iona in 1688, drew a fair and probably a perceptive conclusion : 'Men, manners, habits, buildings, everything different from our own; and if we thought them rude and barbarous, no doubt the people had the same opinion of what belonged to us, and the wonder was mutual'.

The year when the visit was made and the author's name come at the start of each extract. Bibliographical details are listed at the end of the book. For the reader's interest, notes have been added in each chapter on the travellers or on the context in which their accounts were written. The original spelling and punctuation of the writers have been retained. Where additional notes of clarification are needed within passages, I have put these in square brackets. It is the extracts themselves, however, which form the substance of the book and which, I hope, will inform and entertain all who know the Hebrides and, in particular, Iona.

Mairi MacArthur

ST. MARTIN'S CROSS.

FRUITFUL IN CORN AND GRASS

From the systematic Hebridean tour made in 1549 by
Donald Monro, Dean of the Isles, we have a very brief
description of Iona. It is the earliest, so far as we know,
since the time of Columba and his successors. He called it
'ane faire mayne ile...fertil land fruitfull of corne'. The
fertility of the land is mentioned in the three extracts which
follow, from a century or more later, and it is a theme
echoed consistently by many who came later.

The strange account of a doomed family is alluded
to by both Sacheverell and Martin. The tradition of a direct
link back to people living in Columba's time lingered on.
Boswell reported in 1773 that their local guide, unnamed,
claimed descent from a cousin of St. Columba. And when
crofter Malcolm Ferguson gave evidence to the Napier
Commission in 1883 he stated that a family of Blacks (at
Cnoc Cùl Phàil) were said to be the oldest in Iona and that
they had come from Ireland with the Saint. Families did
not, in fact, always stay in one part of the Highlands for
generations; there was considerable movement from place
to place and from time to time. It is unlikely, too, that oral
tradition could last directly from such an early date as the
6th century. What the stories do show, however, is that
Columba and his community were firmly part of the
people's history on the island.

Martin will have been able to speak to them in
Gaelic, their only language at that time, as he was himself a
native of the Hebrides. He had a keen interest in custom
and folklore, hence his notes about the powers associated
with various stones in the Cathedral grounds.

1688 : Dr. W. Sacheverell

I went next to seek the so-much-talked-of town of Sodor. None of the inhabitants had any notion of it but I found a broad pavement about 300 yards long on the South part of the Abbey running to a pretty nunnery and on each side some mean cabins and many ruins of a poor village...

The greatest part of the inhabitants of this village are called Mac-en-Oysters, in English the sons of the officers upon which another story depends, which is firmly believed by all persons here. Columbus *(sic)* brought several servants with him out of Ireland, whom he made officers in his abbey; but they, by their negligence or otherwise, having disobliged him, he prayed they might never exceed the number they then were, which was eight; and though this was 1200 years ago, it is said they never yet were more than eight and rarely fewer than six. I asked the Dean about it and he said it was a standing observation and generally believed. Their offspring continued hereditary servants to the end; and perhaps the good man was afraid to bring too great a charge upon his foundation. They are at present miserably poor, since the ruin of the abbey; one of them pretends to show the monuments and gets some small matter by it.

They seem an innocent, simple people, ignorant and devout; and though they have no minister, they constantly assemble in the great church on Sundays where they spend most part of the day in private devotions.

...

I now began to climb the mountain which secures the abbey from the Western winds. I found the ascent easy with a pleasant mixture of rocks and verdant grass;... All the hilly part is a very good sheep-walk, the lower grounds fruitful and arable, and the corn then ripe and actually reaped, though there was no prospect of harvest in a month after in my part of the country. ...I had then leisure to inquire the number of the inhabitants which I was then informed was about 80 families. ...On the marshes near the sea I saw great herds of cows feeding.

6

1693 : Walter MacFarlane

This Ile...full of little hillocks, pleasant and healthfull with a store of common medicinall herbs naturally growing and some the Monks transplanted thither from other places.... The Ile is fruitfull and has plaine arable ground in good measure, interlayed betwixt the little green hills thereoff. The product and chief commoditie is barley....

circa 1695 : Martin Martin

The east side is all arable and plain, fruitful in corn and grass; the west side is thin and rocky. ...St. Mary's Church here is built in form of a cross... The steeple is pretty large; the doors, windows, etc are curiously carved; the altar is large and of as fine marble as any I ever saw. ...Near St. Columba's tomb is St. Martin's cross... A little further to the west lie the black stones, which are so called, not from their colour, for that is grey, but from the effects that tradition say ensued upon perjury, if any one became guilty of it after swearing on these stones in the usual manner; for an oath made on them was decisive in all controversies.

...

There is a heap of stones on which they us'd to lay the corpse while they dug the grave. There is a stone likewise erected here, concerning which the credulous natives say, that whosoever reaches out his Arm along the Stone three times, in the name of the Father, Son and Holy Ghost will never err in Steering the Helm of a Vessel.

...

There was a tribe here called "Clan vic n'oster", from Ostiarii; for they are said to have been porters. The tradition of these is that before Columbus (sic) died thirty of his family lived then in Iona, and that upon some provocation Columbus entailed a curse upon them, which was that they might all perish to the number of five, and that they might never exceed that number, to which they were accordingly reduced; and ever since, when any woman of the family was in labour, both she and the other four were afraid of death; for if the child that was to be then born did not die, they say one of the five was sure to die; and this they affirm to have been verified on every such occasion successively to this day. I found one only of this tribe living in the isle and both he and the natives of this and of all the Western Isles unanimously declare that this observation never fail'd and all this little family is now extinct except this one poor man.

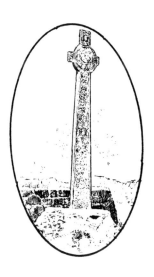

Plate 1 Sithean Mòr (big fairy hill), also known as Angel Hill, with the fine crops noted by visitors in the foreground. (Donald B. MacCulloch, 1930s)

Plate 2 18th century engraving. Cathedral ruins as seen by the early visitors.

FRESH FIELDS FOR INQUIRY

In a biographical sketch of Richard Pococke, Archdeacon of Dublin, we learn that he travelled widely in Europe as a young man, in the 1730s. Later, he planned a visit to Scotland because 'He desired pastures new, fresh fields for inquiry...'. The late 18th century was indeed an age of scientific and intellectual inquiry, when both the natural and the human environment became subjects of great curiosity. The Highlands, geographically remote and culturally distinct, were an obvious challenge.

Several travellers from this time have left us with much valuable detail about the places and people they saw. Dr. John Walker was one example - a gifted botanist and geologist, he also developed expertise in agriculture and its improvement. He undertook a survey for the Commissioners of the Annexed Estates on the natural history, farming, fishing and industry of the islands. He combined this tour with commissions from the Church to investigate religion and education in the same area. He was thus alert to a wide range of matters everywhere he went.

Thomas Pennant was a zoologist whose observant account was widely read. Three editions were published in his lifetime, as was a translation into German. Thomas Garnett, a Professor of Natural Philosophy and Chemistry, took a copy of Pennant with him on his own journey, the object of which was 'to get as perfect an account as possible of every place and everything I saw'.

What kind of society did these gentlemen find when they landed on Iona? It was, first of all, one where the population was rising rapidly. There were probably around 200 people living on the island when Bishop Pococke visited in 1760. Just before the end of the century Garnett noted from the schoolmaster the precise figure of 336. The people lived from the land and the sea. They shared the arable ground, in a system of farming called run-rig, and their cottages were all clustered in one township between the Nunnery and the Cathedral. The rent they paid to the Duke of Argyll was earned from the sale of black cattle and from burning seaweed to make kelp. It was a highly self-sufficient community as Boswell's account, in particular, makes clear. Although the available accommodation was undoubtedly spartan, food - especially dairy produce - was offered generously to visitors. Dr. Johnson was in a minority in treating it with apparent suspicion!

At this period Iona had neither parish church nor resident minister. It came within the large Mull parish of Kilfinichen and Kilviceuen and the minister crossed over periodically to take services. But the people still clung to older beliefs and customs, some of which had supernatural or pagan undertones, as Pococke, Walker and Garnett point out.

The extract dated 1788 is from the diary of a sail in August that year on the cutter *Royal George Revenue*. The hand has been identified as that of John, 1st Marquess of Bute. Later in the same manuscript are fragmentary notes from another journal, dated 12-19 October 1788, from a cruise on the *Loch Fyne*. Again, the entries are not signed but the writer was probably another member of the Bute family. He begins by naming the schoolteacher, whom the 'Society' - ie the Scottish Society for the Propagation of Christian Knowledge (SSPCK) - had appointed when Iona school was first established in 1774. The teacher also acted as Catechist. 'Port Wherry' and 'Port Ourie' in these passages probably resulted from a mishearing of 'Port a'Churaich', the Gaelic name for Bay of the Coracle or Columba's Bay.

1760 : Bishop Pococke

At I-Colm Kill I met Mr. Campbell the Bailie of the Isle of Terre-I, who with great complaisance attended me in seeing everything.

...

There are about thirty-six families on the Island who live in the Village of the Churches. I-Colm Kill is in the district of the neighbouring minister in Mull, who performs service here once a quarter in a private house.

The marble altar...the common people break pieces off from it which they affect to use as a medicine for man or beasts in most Disorders and especially the flux.

At the west end of the Church is a Cross called St.Martin's and to the west of that a higher [one], about which they bury unbaptised children. ...About a quarter of a mile to the South of the town is a little Bay where bodies were always landed which were brought to be buried, and till within this six years Women were always buried in the Nunnery and Men in the Monastery. To the west of it are the foundations of an enclosure about twenty yards square, which they call the Druids' Burial-place.

I went to the south west part of the Island and in half a mile passed by a fine small green hill called Angel Hill, where they bring their horses on the day of St.Michael and All Angels, and run races round it; it is probable this custom took its rise from bringing cattle at that season to be blessed...

In I-Colm Kill, when I went into a poor house with the Bailie of Terr-I a woman brought in a wooden vessel of new Milk and drank to the Bailie who performed the same ceremony to me and so it went round. After we had viewed everything, I was conducted to a house where Eggs, Cheese, Butter and Barley Cake were served and a large bowl of Curds.

1764 : Dr. John Walker

A light sandy soil prevails over the whole Island, which in some places however is very fertile. Upon the Sea Shore especially there are some small Plains, exceedingly pleasant that afford good

Crops of Bear and Oats. The Hills are covered with a fine Verdure and afford a very rich dry pasture for Black Cattle and Sheep. Some of the Hills are arable to the Top but those on the South End of the island are over run with Heath; yet the small Valleys interspersed among them are filled with Grass of finest Quality.

For of the 200 Inhabitants, there is not one, who can either speak English or read the Scriptures, though their little island was for many Centuries one of the chief seats of Religion and Learning in Britain. ... They are all of the lowest Rank, under a Gentleman of the name of Campbell who rents the Island, but they are a civil inoffensive People. They are apparently in great Poverty and yet are happy in having to supply all the wants with which they are acquainted. ...

They have all of them a remarkable Propensity to whatever is marvellous and supernatural. Every Person has the traditional History of Columba with numberless legends, which have been handed down from his monkish Seminary. They are famous for the Second Sight; full of Visions seen either by themselves or others; and have many wild and romantick notions concerning Religion and invisible things. ...Having no opportunity of Publick Worship above three or four times a year, when visited by their Minister, it is their custom to repair on the Sabbath to their Devotions in the ruinous Abbey, to Columba's tomb and to the Chapells of several different Saints.

Their regard is so great for these antient Monuments that it has always been the Custom, before any Person is buried in Icolumbkill to carry the Corpse with great Reverence, round the whole Buildings, which occupy a great Space of Ground. This Practice was for the first time abolished, but a little time before I was there, by the Reverend Mr. Neil MacLeod their present Minister.

It is not at all surprising, however, that the inhabitants of Iona should be remarkable for superstition beyond their neighbours... They are a people whose imagination is evidently the most lively of all their faculties... Their unlimited veneration for antiquity supplies the place of truth in the most marvellous of frightful legends.

1772 : Thomas Pennant

The soil is a compound of sand and comminuted sea shells, mixed with black loam; is very favourable to the growth of bear, natural clover, crowsfoot and daisies. It is in perpetual tillage, and is ploughed thrice before sowing: the crops at this time made a promising appearance, but the seed was committed to the ground at very different times, some I think about the beginning of May and some not three weeks ago. Oats do not succeed here; but flax and potatoes come on very well.

The tenants here run-rig and have the pasturage in common. ...the town, which lies almost close to the Bay of Martyrs...consisting at present of about fifty houses, mostly very mean, thatched with straw of bear pulled up by the roots, and bound tight on the roof with ropes made of heath. Some of the houses that lie a little beyond the rest seemed to have been better constructed than the others, and to have been the mansions of the inhabitants when the place was in a flourishing state, but at present are in a very ruinous condition.

1773 : James Boswell

Upon hearing that Sir Allan Maclean was arrived...the inhabitants - who still consider themselves as people of MacLean, though the Duke of Argyll has at present possession of the ancient estate - ran eagerly to him. We went first to the house of MacDonald, the most substantial man among them. Sir Allan called him the Provost. He had a tolerable hut with higher walls than common and pretty well built with dry stone. The fire was in the middle of the room

The people seemed to be more decently dressed than one usually finds those of their station in the isles. ...They sell about 40 cattle and more than 150 bolls of barley; and what is remarkable they brew a good deal of beer which I could not find was done in any of the other isles. I was told they imported nothing but salt and iron. Salt they might soon make. It is a very fertile island and the people are industrious. They make their own woollen and linen webs, and indeed I suppose everything else, except for any hardware for which they may have occasion. They have no shoes for their horses.

After warming ourselves in Mr. MacDonald's, we were informed that our barn was ready and we repaired to it. There was a fire in the middle of the floor but the smoke was ceased before we went into the barn. We had cuddies and some oysters boiled in butter, that we might say we had fish and oyster sauce. Mr. Johnson ate none of that dish. We had roasted potatoes of which I think he ate one; and he drank a mug of sweet milk. The fire was then carefully removed and good hay was strewed at one end of the barn. Mr. Johnson lay down with all his clothes and his greatcoat on. Sir Allan and I took off our coats and had them laid upon our feet. But we had also a pair of clean sheets which Miss Maclean had put up, and some very good blankets from the village; so that we had a tolerably comfortable bed...

[next morning] Between seven and eight we rose and went to see the ruins. We had for our cicerone ___ who calls himself the descendant of St.Columba's cousin. ...We walked down again to our barn, where breakfast was prepared - milk, cheese, eggs, bread and butter. ...We had a goodly number of the people to launch our boat; and when we sailed or rather rowed off, they took off their bonnets and huzza'd.

1787 : James Bailey

We immediately walked to the village where we soon found the inn or hut where we were to be accommodated for the night. In a place with so little intercourse not much of comfort was to be expected and indeed a more wretched hovel than this can scarcely be conceived. This was but of trifling consideration as we had so many other objects in our thoughts and to make sure of provisions we had brought bread from Mull. Milk at least we might calculate upon but we might have spared our solicitude as neither these nor many other articles were wanting.

Our next care was to search for the person who is seasonally employed by strangers for pointing out and explaining the antiquities of the island and who is the son of the man whom Johnson distinguished as the head man here... We soon met him and found him courteous and obliging; and what was of still greater consequence profoundly skilled in the legendary history of Hy. The truth was he had been presented by some curious visitant with a 'Life of Columba' written I believe in Ireland; so that his narrations were not exclusively limited to oral information. He has also the appointment of schoolmaster and therefore speaks the English language with great facility and with no inconsiderable degree of purity. ...He was never from my side during the whole of my survey of these interesting ruins and on the following morning I had his company in my rambles to different parts of the island.

[After visiting the ruins they returned to the inn for the night.]

Our hostess had not been inattentive to our interests for she had made a large cheese-cake for supper after which we had plentiful beverage of milk.

[Next day they walked to Port a'Churaich and to Dun I, again in the company of their guide.] ...I will not detail the marvellous stories with which the memory of my Cicerone was so amply furnished and with which he took great pains to amuse me; such as that of the punishment of Oran...I shall always however remember the attention of this harmless creature and I hope I did not part with him without demonstrating the sincerity of my obligations.

The greater part of [the island] is arable and a large surplus of grain is annually laid up for exportation. Kelp has also of late years become a very lucrative article as the rocks on the back of the island are peculiarly abundant in the wrack from which it is manufactured. A valuable white fishery has lately been discovered on the coat of Hy and the inhabitants are using considerable exertions for making it productive. The revenue which is drawn by the Duke of Argyll is in a rapid state of augmentation and in process of time he may think it proper to erect more commodious dwellings on this island.

1788 : Marquess of Bute

Went ashore at 11 o'clock and made our entry with the piper playing before us. Visited the Nunnery, from there walked to Port Wherry where having collected all the curiosities the spot afforded we crossed over to the West of the island and following the sands till nearly opposite the town we took a strait direction which brought us to a hill called Angel Hill, formerly a sacred spot and the ruins of a chapel are still to be seen. Returning afternoon to the town, I proceeded to the churchyard and turned as directed the stones on one grave and on another, which act of piety commands according to tradition all possible luck.

...Port Martyr where the bodies of great men are said to have been landed, a small hillock adjoining is marked as the spot where the coffin was deposited previous to the procession taking place. Near this spot you find an old burying used by the Druids previous to Columba's arrival and from that time to this very day the spot being 50 feet square is preserved with the most reverential respect. It is covered with the finest verdure under which appears two feet of the richest mold, under that a sand that preserves the bones, a fact I ascertained by digging a proper depth and bringing away the bone of a toe. At Port Ourie you are shown two heaps of stone marking the length of Columba's vessel. ...Near this I heard for the first time an earse song performed by the women who were burning kelp, a melancholy ditty.

Having completed my survey and it being past eight I prepared to go on board but first went into the school room, the door of which was four foot high, and having heard a few boys and girls read in wonderfully good English the Bible I gave them a trifle each and, distributing tobacco to all the men, I took boat.

Robert Colquhoun - sent by the Society - £10...now 25 scholars. He pays £2 out of his salary to make it up to assistant. Teaches Gallic and English, writing and five rules of arithmetic. ...once in two years list of souls renewed for minister by catechist who every Sunday convenes the people by order to Society, who reads the scriptures, prayer ordered by them, and sings psalms in

18

the Gallic...last list made in March 1788 - then 285 souls - natives increasing. Rent paid the Duke about £180 - product cattle, kelp and barley.

Drovers come at Whitsuntide - cattle £3 to £5 - horses bred in island, best worth 6 guineas. Salt ling and cod for themselves - no game - lobsters and crabs - great use of milk - wild geese in autumn - no fruit of any sort... Brogues are made - women make the stockings and plaid - men the belts - taylor in Mull comes when wanted - pedlars from all quarters every month who supply their other wants and drain the money.

1798 : Thomas Garnett

We sailed between Icolmkill and a small island called the Isle of Nuns; and as we approached the former we saw a considerable number of kelp-makers at work on the shore.

...

The number of inhabitants in the island at this time was 336...it seems a very healthy place, notwithstanding the poverty of the inhabitants. ...The island is divided into two districts and the cattle in each are herded by a common herd... The inhabitants of this island cannot, however, be praised for their industry, being by no means fond of agriculture, which is owing to their being tenants at will, or having no leases of their farms. Where there is any arable ground, the farmers run-rig as it is called...This island from the nature of its soil, seems much more capable of improvement by cultivation than any part of Mull; but this can never take place to any considerable extent till the tenants have leases and comfortable cottages, instead of the wretched hovels which they inhabit. ...

Oats, barley and some flax are cultivated here and potatoes grow remarkably well. Their method of sowing barley is singular: the seed is sown before the ground is ploughed and they then plough the ground over it. This prevents the grain from being bared by high winds, which are often known to drift the sandy soil off it. This mode, which was undoubtedly introduced by necessity, answers very well. The potatoes are manured by sea ware collected during the winter. ...

They still retain some opinions handed down by their ancestors, perhaps from the times of the Druids. In particular they believe that the spirit of the last person that was buried watches round the church-yard till another is interred, to whom he delivers his charge. There is a person in the island by the name of Innis, who pretends to cure scrofula by touching. He is a seventh son...he asks no fee and it is believed that if he did there would be no cure. He is often sent for out of the island...

Here are some persons who can repeat several of the Celtic poems of Ossian and other bards. The schoolmaster told me he could repeat a very long one on the death of Oscar, which was taught him by his grandfather.

FELLOW PEDESTRIAN TOURISTS

George Douglas's experience in Oban illustrates the increasingly busy role of the town by the start of the 19th century, as the trek westwards grew in popularity. A few years later Sir John Carr was to call Oban 'the great disembarking port for Mull, Staffa and Iona'. Means of transport was on foot, horseback and by small boat. Douglas's party sailed to Aros in Mull on a kelp vessel belonging to MacDonald of Staffa, whom one of them evidently knew. They then rode overland to Loch na Keal where a boat with four oarsmen met them.

Douglas mentions the Hon. Mrs.Sarah Murray of Kensington, also in Oban when he arrived. Her first visit to the Hebrides that year was followed up two years later by a longer trip, from which the second extract comes. Mrs. Murray's *Guide* is an early example of a new kind of account - one aimed particularly at fellow travellers. An intrepid explorer, she recorded with evident zest that she was the ninth female stranger to visit Staffa but the first to do so 'valiantly alone'. One of her aims was to give readers an array of practical advice - the type of carriage to choose, what baggage to take, the best routes and inns, where to hire horses and so on.

History was not, perhaps, her forte. She seemed to believe, for example, that Columba had built the Nunnery which in fact dates from the 13th century. Her writing is lively and informative, however, on a whole range of social and cultural matters. The reference to the subdivision of the farming land into thirty holdings corroborates other evidence that, in or around this date of 1802, the Duke created individual crofts for his tenants. From this time, too, those who were allocated crofts moved out of the central village to build houses on their own land. The village was then relocated in a main street facing the sea, as we know it today.

The extract from Douglas is the first in this collection to mention the selling of pebbles and shells. Children were especially good at pursuing this trade, to the amusement of some visitors and the annoyance of others. As befitted her adventurous nature, Mrs. Murray opted to go and find her own mementoes, at the Marble Quarry and at Port a'Churaich. We join her narrative after she had ridden through Glen More and right down the Ross of Mull. She was accompanied to Iona by the minister, Mr. Campbell, and some of his family, with whom she had spent the previous night at Bunessan.

1800 : George Douglas

[Oban] Every apartment of the small inn occupied by tourists. ...the Hon. Mr. Ward is at present here with a large party and the Hon. Mrs. Murray is also exercising her graphic talents in an adjoining lodging. Mr. Stevenson the Engineer too and some other people occupy a part of the house and we consider ourselves lucky under such circumstances in getting any accommodation whatever. I find that my friend Auchterlony with his fellow Pedestrian tourists were here two days ago and seem much delighted with their excursions.

...

Our boatmen proved very intelligent companions and entertained us with Gaelic songs, ancient legends etc as we pursued our watery course toward the island of Icolmkill. When we landed we were received by nearly the whole population with the schoolmaster at their head and much pestered by some to purchase the shells and specimens of soft green pebbles, resembling the Chinese soap stone, which abound on this coast...

[At the ruins] We thoughtlessly lifted three curious round stones and were about to toss them to and from each other when we were gravely entreated by the schoolmaster to desist from such unhallowed sport as he assured us that tradition had predicted the end of the world when the said stones were completely worn away by the handling of strangers.

1802 : Sarah Murray

A boat had been ordered to meet us at the point of Ross, opposite the harbour near the town in I-Ona. The day, from a very doubtful morning, became as fine as possible, and quite calm; we therefore embarked with pleasure, leaving our horses to get what food they could amongst the granite masses until our return. We crossed the Sound to procure an addition of two rowers, that we might go by sea to Port-a-Churaich, so called because Saint Columba first landed on I-Ona in his wicker boat at that small bay on the south side of the island. ...We rowed as near the shore as possible, and a bold shore of rocks it is, particularly near the marble quarry where vast cliffs of marble rise in irregular masses from the sea to a great height.

The young men of our party and three of the boatmen ran up and down the broken points and sides of these tremendous cliffs like goats; it was quite terrifying to look at them. They reached the marble quarry and returned to the boat laden with marble of three kinds; pure white, white veined with bright light green and a light gray or rather dove colour. The quarry was worked only for a short time; why it was discontinued I cannot say.

When we came near the southern point of I-Ona the rocks became wonderfully bold and sublime; innumerable rocky islands too are scattered near to Port-a-Churaich... We entered it peaceably and landed on the sloping pebbly beach, and there I picked up gray pebbles beautifully marked; fine lapis nephriticus; jaspers, green mixed with red; serpentine stone, gray and other porphyries; pure white marble and many other rare stones, of which I do not know the names, all rounded and in some degree polished.

...

Part of the ground around the Cathedral, when I was at I-Ona, was planted with potatoes and other vegetables; the rest of it was over-run with the most luxuriant weeds and wild plants I ever beheld. ...Whilst I was fighting with the stubborn wild plants (up to my waist), my friend Mr. Campbell (who is the minister of Ross of which parish I-Ona is a part) asked me by which race of men I would choose to sleep were death to seize me in I-Ona... By those of Scotland undoubtedly was my choice. The question was not unaptly put for had death taken a fancy to my house of clay while wandering in I-Ona there my bones must have pulverised, for the superstition of the inhabitants is such that for ages no corpse has been suffered without force to be carried out of that island; for as long as that custom is maintained, say they, no I-Onian can be drowned in the Sound between I and Ross so that an absolute embargo is laid on the bodies of all human beings who die in I-Columbkill.

The inhabitants also believe (and the same belief pervades the lower order of people in other parts of the parish of Ross) that the last person buried keeps watch around the burying ground until another body is interred...

I-Ona to its proprietor, the Duke of Argyle, is worth about one hundred and forty pounds a year; consisting of two equal farms, and these are subdivided into about thirty farms. ...The soil of it is very productive of barley, oats and potatoes; the profit arising from the latter is often sufficient to pay the whole rent of a farm.

There are no trees on the island, nor fuel of any sort. At the proper season the inhabitants cross over to Ross where they find plenty of peat mosses. From these mosses or black bogs, they cut, dry and pile vast quantities of peat and let them remain in stacks upon the mosses until completely fit for use; they then set all their boats and hands to work to convey their yearly store ·of fuel across the Sound to their houses.

... After visiting the ruins of the cathedral and nunnery, and surveying the ancient tombs of great men long forgotten, our party reached the inn, not equal to a hotel, but by no means in so despicable a state as when Dr. Garnett and Mr. Watts were in danger of being suffocated with laughter, excited by the crowing of a young cock perched over their heads. Since that time the public room in the inn at I-Ona has acquired a new ceiling which now excludes the rain... the room was dry and as clean as I expected to find it...there were two beds in it....

The good woman at the inn at I-Ona, when we returned from our long and fatiquing peregrination, furnished us with a meal of fine fish and excellent potatoes; hunger added the best of sauce.

Plate 3 Carved stones and grave slabs in the Rèilig Orain, with the ruins of St. Oran's Chapel and the Cathedral beyond, 1890s.

Plate 4 Ferry under sail from Iona to Fionnphort, around the turn of this century.

Plate 5 Visitors searching for pebbles on the Machair shore, 1890s. Serpentine, or 'greenstone', has always been especially prized.

TRIP IT ON THE LIGHT FANTASTIC TOE

The three extracts which follow all describe dancing, either in honour of or along with visitors to the island. The first two, in particular, remind us that music, song and dance were a vital part of popular culture everywhere in the Highlands. They contributed to the people's well-being and these writers' appreciation of this is unusual. Most observers assessed the locals' prosperity and contentment in material terms alone and, naturally, found those poor in comparison with their own societies. Few took the trouble to enquire further how the people lived and entertained themselves. This barrier was certainly breached by the anonymous gentleman's party, by Necker de Saussure and - who knows? - by others who have gone unrecorded. For the piper in the first extract was almost certainly Archibald MacArthur from Ulva, trained by the famous Donald MacCrummin of Skye. MacArthur was piper to Ronald MacDonald, Laird of Staffa, and often accompanied visitors to Staffa and Iona. The islanders were clearly glad to see him!

1806 : Anonymous

The view of Iona from the sea is very picturesque. The south east side exhibits a beautiful variety; an extent of plain a little elevated above the water and almost covered with the ruins of the sacred buildings and a village of huts. ...We landed at a creek close by the village. ...Our arrival was greeted by a number of people on the beach, who were attracted by our piper's music. For as soon as he got within hearing of the island he had struck up a pibroch with all his vigour and continued his music till we landed. He then ranged us behind him and we were marched single file through the village to the tune of some favourite highland air, apparently to the great delight of the natives. He conducted us to a flat at the east end of the village where he called a halt and we were introduced in great form to the schoolmaster, the *king* of the island. This great personage is the *Cicerone* of the place. He has a salary of £15 a year from the society for propagating christian knowledge and £9 from the Duke of Argyle and a free house. He had then about 30 scholars but in spring has sometimes upwards of 70. We here left the piper to amuse the villagers and followed the schoolmaster to the ruins.

...

[They found the buildings very impressive and used Dr.Johnson's words to describe their feelings of awe and wonder. Meanwhile, the piper was still playing...] It was the more grateful to them [the villagers] as, though the bagpipe is a native of the Highlands, the whole island does not at present afford a performer on that instrument. They became at last so exhilarated that they began to 'trip it on the light fantastic toe' and when we returned dancing was 'the order of the day'. One of our boatmen, a nice young man of the name of Allan MacInnes, was master of ceremonies and to do him justice he did his duty most dexterously.

We looked on for some time but at last, observing four ladies propose to dance a reel by themselves, our gallantry took the alarm and we immediately joined the jovial crew. With this frankness added to a roving commission with which we had despatched Allan to the Alehouse for whisky, the villagers seemed much pleased. It is amazing how many good looking girls there were in the company, several of them would have done honour to the streets of Edinburgh. ...There was one girl in particular very pretty, Miss Effy McLean, to whom Wilson and I paid great court. ...This girl was really good looking and was Allan's sweetheart.

...We concluded each reel in the good old fashion of kissing our partners, a fashion that I am sorry to see has in our part of the country gone into disuse.

Allan now returned with the whisky with which we made a forum of grog in a large punch bowl. ...We first helped our partners and then distributed it among the spectators who now amounted to upwards of 200, the whole inhabitants in the place.

There occurred a circumstance that afforded us much amusement at poor Wilson's expense. An old ugly woman observed him, besides kissing his partner, slip some money into her hand at the end of the reel. Wishing to have some but despairing to be asked out as a partner, she thought the only way she could accomplish her purpose was by craving him for some. She did not understand English so made her request in Gaelic. Wilson was as ignorant of her language as she was of his and mistook the request as for a kiss. This he was gallant enough not to refuse and throwing his arms around her weathered trunk gave her a hearty smack. The woman seemed a good deal surprised and all those who understood her lingo and witnessed the scene burst into a loud laugh, in which we and Wilson himself very good naturedly joined after the object of the request had been explained. He then satisfied the woman in the way she wanted.

Among the group of dancers there was a couple whom the rest of the company would not associate with. They were Irish of profligate character who had lately come to Iona and were held in detestation by all the old inhabitants. When we were about to depart the man came up to Mr. Brown and offered him for sale what he averred was a great curiosity, a sacred relic from the tomb of Saint Oran.

It is a sort of trade among the children here to collect pebbles and sell them to strangers. They came around us in dozens, some of them in the true garb of nature, with pebbles in their hands pressing us to bargain with them. They had none of any value but as they did not ask an exorbitant price we, particularly Wilson, made some purchases.

After regaling the inhabitants with another bowl of grog and taking an affectionate farewell of the nymphs, particularly of Effy, we left the island with sensations very different from what I expected to have felt. The inhabitants seemed vastly taken with us and as we were going off gave us three cheers which salute we returned with a discharge of our musquet. ...Will we be accused of presumption if we hint that the year 1806 will be long cherished in Iona under the title of the year that strangers from Ulva treated them with a ball.

[On the return the party visited MacKinnon's Cave in Mull and the island of Inchkenneth. As night fell, the indefatigable piper was still playing and was persuaded to stop only when they threatened to throw him bags and all into the sea.] ...The bagpipe is not an unpleasant instrument at a distance, in Fingals Cave it is even harmonious, but there is no bearing for any length of time the drone close to your ear.

This was one of the pleasantest and best spent days of my life. ...It is but few days in a lifetime that you meet with an assemblage of such interesting objects as what this afforded. Nature upon the most magnificent scale in Staffa and MacKinnon's Cave, splendid remains sacred to religion and virtue in Iona, and the native simplicity and rustic happiness of its present inhabitants.

1807 : L. A. Necker de Saussure

A little before we arrived the piper, according to custom, played one of the marches of the MacDonalds and soon a number of the inhabitants, men women and children, sallied forth; while some remained at the door of their huts and others advanced to the shore to see us land. We leaped on the shore and were presently surrounded by a multitude of children presenting us small pebbles of a yellow serpentine, hard and transparent, which they gather on the sea shore.

...at present Icolmkill possesses a school; the master who directs it appears to be a well informed man. I was agreeably surprised to hear him speak of Mont Blanc in Switzerland, of its ice and perpetual snows and address to me some very sensible questions on objects so remote from these districts.

We promised to reward our boatmen for their past zeal, by treating them with a dance at Iona in the evening, as dancing is the favourite amusement of the Hebrideans of all ages. They brought us a fiddler, and we invited the inhabitants of the village to a dance in our hut. We much admired the gaiety, the liveliness of their national dances and the address with with they avoided the deep holes of the ground on which they leaped. The luxury of floors is unknown here and in the interior of the houses the inhabitants still tread on damp and rough soil.

We plied the dancers with toddy and in the intervals between the reels they sung several Gaelic songs in full chorus. Although these songs, as well as those we heard on the sea, consisted of a solo and chorus, they differed little in the rhyme but the words were different; the airs composed to be sung on the water, and accompanied by the noise of the oars, are called jorrams *(sic)*, the others bear the name of Oran luathaidh and are only sung on land to amuse the workmen in their labours; they are a species of ballads, or recitations of adventures, sometimes heroic or tragical, and at other times of a comic and burlesque character.

The men and women seated themselves in a circle and joined hands or held, in couples, the end of handkerchief with which they kept time during the chorus. Two of our boatmen who were the leaders made all kinds of grimaces and apish tricks whilst singing, striking themselves on the head one against the other with all the dexterity of Italian buffoons, while the rest of the company were convulsed with laughter. This scene greatly amused us and we were astonished to see, under so foggy an atmosphere, in so dreary a climate, a people animated by that gaiety and cheerfulness which we are apt to attribute exclusively to those nations who inhabit the delightful countries of the South of Europe.

1807 : Sir John Carr

Two of our party had been at Iona a short time before with the Duke of Argyll, whose presence produced almost as great a sensation as if St.Columba attended by St. Patrick and St. Bridget had risen from his tomb to revisit this his favourite island. His

Grace is the great chieftain of the place and during a century it has never been so honoured. All the population crowded to the shore when the Duke and his party landed, to whom they offered some of the finest pebbles found on the island, many of which are very beautiful. The tombs of the Scottish and Irish kings had been cleaned of their super-incumbent loads of cattle-dung and duly washed and scrubbed.

The schoolmaster, the greatest personage upon the island, had 'wasted the midnight oil' in preparing a speech with which to address the Duke; but alas! like many an unpractised orator, when the long looked for opportunity arrived the powers of his memory melted away and he stood in a state of pale and trembling stupefaction. The men and women in fine white mob caps, and without shoes or stockings, danced an Iona fandango before the Duke whilst the children pressed forward to touch his coat.

THE EQUALITY OF POVERTY

Material conditions were, of course, hard. The low thatched cottages of the period, though sturdy enough, were dark and damp. The lack of a doctor in the area also caused problems at times, as the Teignmouth party witnessed. Later, in 1843, the minister was to state to the Poor Law Inquiry Commission that the nearest doctor for his parishioners was at Torloisk, in north-west Mull, and that he himself had had to vaccinate children as a result.

1826 : Bernard Ducos

The steamboat stops and we disembark with the help of the launch. The beach on which it deposits us is a confused mass of huge flints and rocks. Beyond and quite far off emerges a row of dilapidated cottages with a narrow winding path in front, strewn with sharp stones. We reach it with great difficulty, not without stumbling and taking the risk of a hard fall. Our arrival arouses the curiosity of the inhabitants. Women run to the doorways. We walk surrounded by children clothed in rags. The men look at us sideways, surreptitiously and as if they reproach us for being happier, or less unhappy, than they are.

One of them comes forward. He has better clothes; his manner is less wild: it is the *cicerone* of the place. He offers to guide us and we follow. On the way to the ruins I notice in one of the huts of this miserable village a young, tall, beautiful woman. She has Greek features, dark eyes, a sad expression. Her hair is caught up on top of her head. She wears a shawl over her blouse and a short soot-coloured skirt. Her legs and feet are bare and dirty. I ask permission to visit her house and, though she speaks only Gaelic, she understands and invites me in. It is just a single room between four walls of mud, straw, branches and clumps of dried turf. There is no window or paved floor. Daylight comes in by the door. In the centre, set against two stones, clods of peat smoulder. The smoke goes out through the roof, made of heather roots and reeds, bound with sea grasses and held down with pebbles.

The length of this rustic home, on two pallets strewn with bracken and other brittle plants, trail scraps of woollen blanket. An old woman crouched on her heels gives out a little grain to hens and ducks. In a corner pigs eat vegetable peelings. A layer of dung, several inches thick, covers the ground. This cottage is not the poorest nor the least cared for. They are all alike; it is the equality of poverty. I gave some money to the young woman who showed extreme gratitude... I had not noticed one of our passengers, from Glasgow, an educated and well-mannered man who witnessed this silent scene. 'What misery!' I said, turning back to him. 'They are used to it' he replied with an indifferent smile.

1825 : J.E. Bowman

This very humble and dirty village is now the abode only of Hebridean fishermen and kelp makers; we entered one of the huts to beg a little water to moisten our parched palates; it was smoky dark and squalid in the extreme yet its poor inhabitants wore the smile of content and were civil and obliging, according to our wishes, expressed by signs for they did not understand our wishes.

1827 : Lord Teignmouth

Of the want of surgical assistance we witnessed a melancholy proof. The schoolmaster, our guide, anxiously enquired of us when we landed whether a professional man was of our party and soon conducted us to a cottage where a fisherman displayed an arm dreadfully swollen in consequence of the prick of a fin of a gurnet; ...This poor fellow subsequently suffered amputation of the finger, but whether his life was preserved we did not hear. The party from the steam-vessel furnished medicines and subscribed to procure the assistance of a surgeon from Tobermory.

SUMMER TOURS IN SCOTLAND.

THE ROYAL ROUTE.

GLASGOW AND THE HIGHLANDS,

Via Crinan and Caledonian Canals.

TOURIST'S SPECIAL Cabin Tickets issued during the Season, Giving the *privilege* of the run of *all the undernamed Steamers to any part of the Highlands* where they may call at during the time specified. For One Week, £3 ; or Two Weeks, £5.

THE ROYAL MAIL STEAMERS WITH PASSENGERS ONLY.	NEW STEAM-SHIP "CLAYMORE" OR "CLANSMAN" A WEEK'S TOUR, TO MULL, SKYE, & STORNOWAY.	THE ROYAL MAIL STEAMERS WITH GOODS & PASSENGERS.
Columba. Gondolier. Iona. Glengarry. Chevalier. Glencoe. Mountaineer. Linnet. Pioneer. Lochawe. AND Queen of the Lake.	Cabin Fare, with first-class sleeping accommodation, 45/; or including meals, 80/. The route is through scenery rich in historical interest and un-equalled for grandeur and variety. These vessels leave Glasgow every Monday and Thursday about 12 noon, and Greenock about 5 p.m.	Claymore (New Steam-Ship). Clansman. Lochiel. Clydesdale. Fingal. Staffa. Cygnet. Islay. Plover. AND Inveraray Castle.

The Steam-Ship STAFFA leaves Glasgow every Monday at 12 noon and Greenock at 4 p.m., for Inverness and Back, leaving Inverness every Thursday morning ; Cabin Fare for the Trip, with First-class Sleeping Accommodation. 30/ ; or including Meals, 56/.

THE ROYAL MAIL SWIFT PASSENGER STEAMER

"COLUMBA" OR "IONA"

Sails daily from May till October, from Glasgow at 7 A.M., and from Greenock about 9 A.M., in connection with Express Trains from London and the South, Edinburgh. and Glasgow, &c., for KYLES OF BUTE, TARBERT, and ARDRISHAIG, conveying Passengers for OBAN, GLENCOE, INVERNESS, LOCHAWE, STAFFA and IONA, MULL, SKYE, GAIRLOCH, STORNOWAY, &c., &c.

A WHOLE DAY'S SAIL BY THE "COLUMBA" OR "IONA."
From Glasgow to Ardrishaig and Back (180 miles)

CABIN FARE,   ...   6/.   or including Breakfast, Dinner and Tea   12/.
FORE CABIN FARE, ...   3/6.   do.   do.,   do.   do.   7/.

OFFICIAL GUIDE BOOK, 3D.; ILLUSTRATED, 6D.; CLOTH GILT, 1s.

Time Bill, Map and List of Fares, sent free on application to the Owner,

DAVID MACBRAYNE, 119 HOPE STREET, GLASGOW.

Plate 6 Advertisement from a guidebook of 1882, during the heyday of the West coast steamship era.

A CARGO OF TOURISTS

1832 : James Johnson

The chief articles of importation are a cargo of tourists, twice a week in summer to see the mouldering ruins of the isle - their exports are little more than variegated pebbles, sold by the children at sixpence a lot and legendary tales rehearsed by Allan Maclean, the village pedagogue, mystagogue and antiquary at nearly the same rate. ...Iona was, in short, the Palestine of the North, the Rome of Ireland and Scotland.

> The opening of the steamboat era in the 1820s quickly made the road to the isles faster, easier and ever more popular. The first commercial sail to Iona was probably that of the *Comet*, on a trip from Fort William in July 1822 with 'upwards of fifty ladies and gentlemen' (*Inverness Courier*). By the end of the decade several different operators were vying for summer custom in West Highland waters. Many services began from the Clyde but Oban too became an increasingly busy point on the route.
>
> The above writer, James Johnson, captured the scene there vividly in 1832 and, although not directly about Iona, his description is worth quoting further for the atmosphere it conveys. The bustle and excitement will have been experienced by many of those who then went on to visit the island:

Oban *is* on a small scale in the West what Ormuz *was* on a large scale in the East. It is the commercial and touristical centre of the Highlands, the Islands and the Lowlands... On two days of the week and at certain hours of the day, three steamers and a stage coach are seen approaching the modern Ormuz from the four cardinal points of the compass... The advent of four such important caravans produces as great a *sensation* in Oban as the arrival of a fleet of Indiamen formerly did in St. Helena; and not merely sensation but motion also.

The whole of Oban is instantly roused from torpor to activity, from listless ennui to fervid excitement. The innkeepers are all on the alert, while the scouts, videttes and purveyors of the rival hotels are on active service and full pay. ...Meanwhile, the contents of the steamers - men, women, children, sheep, poultry, pigs, dogs, salmon, herrings, cakes, trunks, bags, baskets, hampers, books, portfolios, maps, guns, fishing tackle and thousands of other articles are in rapid transit from vessel to vessel - from steamer to coach and from coach to steamer under such a conclatteration of tongues (for language is out of the question) as was never heard round the Tower of Babel...

In a few minutes all is order and harmony in the thriving port of Oban. ...As they converged a few hours previously from the four winds to the central mart or exchange of Oban, they now diverge like radii from the centre in quest of new scenes and fresh sources of excitement.

Allan MacLean, schoolmaster on Iona for more than forty years, has already featured in these extracts in his other guise of *Cicerone* or guide to the antiquities. The range of Latin names John MacCulloch gives him may seem a little exaggerated, but there is no doubt that he was a key figure in the community. From school inspector reports we know that he was a good and dedicated teacher. In local tradition his name lived on as Ailean Sgoilear (scholar Allan) and a granite obelisk commemorating him was erected in the Rèilig Orain in 1880. Visitors generally found him talkative, attentive, knowledgeable - and vigilant in his duties. It appears that the cargoes of tourists were bringing a greater risk of theft or damage to the historic stones. Of course, tourists had a positive impact too. They brought luxuries such as tobacco, they took away local produce, they bought pebbles and more pebbles... And as MacCulloch notes ironically, the local boys knew that the visitors had heard of, and enjoyed, the custom of turning the Clach na Bràth or Judgement Day Stones - even although, by so doing, they were said to be hastening the end of the world!

There are several references to the church and church-going. After 1828 Iona had its own parish church and manse, designed by Thomas Telford as part of the Parliamentary scheme to build extra places of worship in the Highlands and Islands. A further change came in 1843 with the split in the Church of Scotland, usually known as the Disruption. Around half the parishioners broke away to form a Free Church congregation. At first they were forced to meet in the open air, as G.F. Boyle reported, until 1849 when they were permitted by the Duke of Argyll to build their own church at Martyrs Bay.

circa 1811-1819 : Dr. John MacCulloch

Among the ruins of the Monastery were the Sacred Black Stones; but they are no longer to be found. Honest old Maclean, the Mystagogue of the place, was far from being an adept in the secrets of his trade; though combining within himself the joint offices of Coquinarious, Gardinarius, Portarius, Cellerarius, Eleemosynarius and Sacrista.

[the Clach na Bràth, said to have consisted originally of 3 globes of white marble, placed in 3 basins...] A single stone, which the boys of the village take care to preserve, now serves the same purpose; although it seems to be forgotten that it should be turned three times around in the direction of the sun. When this globe is worn out, its great prototype will also be expended; though what particular interest anyone can have in putting an end to the world, is not very intelligible; unless it be to try whether Iona will continue to swim, amid the general wreck of all things.

1835 : Robert Carruthers

Iona, however, is still the Iona of Johnson. Its ruins constitute its riches; and, save that the well-directed bounty of government has graced it with a church, the appearance of the island is the same.

We approached it on a lovely afternoon in summer. The steam-boat had left Oban crowded with tourists - some from America, two Germans and a whole legion of 'the Sassenach'. The quiet beauty of the scene subdued the whole into silence - even the Americans who had *bored* us about their magnificent rivers and steam-boats sailing twenty-five miles an hour. The sea was literally like a sheet of molten gold or silver.

As our vessel drew up to the usual landing-place, every cottage sent forth its inmates, young and old, and the beach was lined with spectators. ...at their head was an old man, with keen eye and stentorian voice, who bawled out that he was the guide and would show the ruins. This declaration was denied by such of the people as could speak English, who stated that the schoolmaster was the true guide and would soon be on the spot. In a few minutes a little round-face man appeared, his chin new reaped, and on his head a smart beaver-hat that shone conspicuously among the bare heads or blue bonnets of the fishermen. He had a staff in one hand and a little book, 'The Historical Account of Iona' in the other. One of the passengers, to flatter the old man, asked him if he was the author of the work. He said he was not, but added with complacency: 'I am of the same clan, the Macleans, and I have some copies to sell'. He then entered on his task of cicerone, which he said he had exercised for forty years on the island.

...

The schoolmaster has seventy scholars daily. Neither a doctor nor lawyer has yet taken root in the island; but Mull is not more than half a mile distant and the Sound is generally navigable. The new Presbyterian church (the Catholic faith cannot now number a single adherent here) is an inestimable benefit to the people, who had formerly only a chance sermon preached from rock or tent by the clergyman of Mull. As we surveyed the church, and the neat parsonage and cultivated garden of the minister of Iona, we were strongly reminded of the incalculable advantages which are conferred on such remote places by a national religious establishment.

1831 : Lumsden

Although the inhabitants are extremely poor, their religious attainments are remarkable. When a stranger lands the first thing they solicit is tobacco, which is esteemed a great luxury. They are polite; and one of their customs is, when passing a person who is in the act of milking a cow, a quantity of milk is offered gratis. The cows and pigs of the island are of a black colour.

The waulking of cloth here, as a substitute for the fulling mill, and by females who sing in chorus and whose notes are raised in proportion to the time engaged at it, is truly curious. Grinding corn between stones or querns, as in ancient times...is still practised in this quarter.

> Before a slipway was built in 1850 the usual landing-place on Iona was at the Carraig Fhada (long rock) which juts out from the bay below the village. If visitors were not sure-footed, it could be a damp and dicey business, as these passengers from the paddle-steamer *The Highlander* found out...

1837 : Sir George Head

Sometimes it was necessary to step across deep chasms, with no better footing on the opposite side than a rudely pointed fragment of stone; at others we proceeded along apparently flat, even pavement, abounding in watery snares for the unwary, and from which in fact caution the most vigilant was insufficient. Here some of the party dropped mid-leg deep into hidden pools, covered deceitfully by the broad slippery leaves of seaweed; others, squeezing under their feet bloated bags or cists attached to some marine plants, squirted water as high as their own or some neighbours' heads... and one or two persons, too confident in their activity, rolled over on their backs and got a sound ducking.

A group of children, chiefly little girls, each with a plate in her hand containing pebbles and shells for sale, had already collected on the shore and were standing in a line to receive us.

On boarding a steam-boat at Oban, bound for Tobermory, the Rev. C.H. Townshend drew a colourful pen portrait of his fellow travellers - a French marquis, three sketchers, a young woman eccentrically dressed, a portly dame enveloped in gold jewellery who was drinking a tumbler of foaming ale with great satisfaction, and a young man with long yellow locks who turned out to be a keen geologist.

Bad weather prevented the steamer from continuing to Staffa and Iona, from Tobermory, but the writer's party decided to disembark there and hire a local boat the next day. A Sandy MacLean obliged them, at a cost of £4 for the trip. They were much impressed by Staffa, likening Fingals Cave to 'a great Indian wigwam' with its roof the island's grassy top, and then proceeded to Iona.

1840 : Chauncy H. Townshend

Even before we touched land we were besieged by a troop of half-naked amphibious-looking boys, who emulously presented to our notice plateful of Iona pebbles... At length the nuisance became so intolerable that we were forced to turn and face the enemy and, charging them with our sticks, compelled them to retire to a respectful distance.

The ruins of the Cathedral are extremely picturesque and some old richly-carved crosses in front of them are irresistibly tempting to a sketcher. While we were drawing one of these, a little pale-looking old man came up, and looking over my shoulder said, 'That which many men and horses could not move, you will carry away with you in your book',... We soon found that he was the schoolmaster of Iona, a well-known personage, celebrated in the guide-books, and himself guide to the antiquities of the island. He was, at this present, engaged in overlooking one or two haymakers, who were carrying their operations round about the Cathedral, whose sacred precincts, small as they are, were turned to good account and were rented, as he told us, by himself.

He, however, left his occupation to attend us over the ruins in which he seemed to take all the pride and interest of a personal profession. To his influence, it appears, much of their present good state of preservation is owing. He had caused walls to be propped, rubbish to be cleared away, and many a beautiful old fragment to be brought to light. So strong was his feeling for his darling ruins that he could not speak with any patience of an Englishman having clandestinely carried off one of the figures that graced a tomb. I liked the old man, his energy and simplicity which was quite child-like. ...Among other matters he gave us an animated account of having visited Iona in company with Legh Richmond...of whom he spoke with extreme admiration. ...I was pleased with the conduct of the schoolmaster when we offered him half a crown for his services. He would not take so much...we could not press on him more than two shillings. Hear this, ye who say that the Scotch are grasping!

The schoolmaster had at first said that he was sure we could be accommodated at the manse but on inquiry he found that the clergyman had guests staying with him and that all his beds were occupied. There was a little inn, to be sure, but its appearance was anything but inviting. Under these circumstances we determined on sleeping on board the cutter.

1841 : James Wilson

The view round [the Cathedral] is varied and interesting and on this occasion was enlivened by groups of country people all in their best attire, some seated on grassy mounds, reposing after their morning journey, others lounging about the cottage doors or interchanging friendly greetings with their country cousins.

We were well pleased to find that the present Duke of Argyll has shown a praiseworthy interest in these long neglected relics of bygone ages.... ...constructing protecting walls and accrediting one or more natives to exercise a vigorous surveillance on all intruders, especially as carry bags and hammers. The Lady E__ C__ lately informed us that a couple of years have not elapsed since a fingering knave of a mineralogist knocked off poor Abbot MacKinnon's nose.

As we returned from the Cathedral, we met the country people in decent, well-dressed knots, and 'sprinklings of blithe company' congregating upon the village in their way to church, but as we were under the necessity of clearing the Sound before the turn of the tide (and might not perhaps have made much of a Gaelic service at any rate) we got under weigh at a rather graceless hour, though with a fine free wind, for Oban.

1844 : G. F. Boyle

The appearance of the island of Iona is in no respect remarkable...The soils appear unproductive, the shore is rocky, the habitations are few and dirty. The population consists chiefly of fishermen and numbers about 500...

A pilot boat boarded us and we rowed on shore.... The boat was large and dirty and was rowed by two men, a little boy was along with them habited in a kilt. The Cathedral church has a striking appearance from the water and gives a religious character to the surrounding waste.... We landed on the rocks and were immediately beset with troops of children, boys and girls, eager to sell pebbles. We bought a few which seemd to please them. Our next inquiry was for the *cicerone* of the place. He soon appeared with his bunch of keys.

...In the burying ground of the kings near the chapel of St.Oran is a sort of sentry-box, from which a non-intrusion minister preaches to his followers, 'the church question' as our guide said, 'having penetrated even into these remote districts'. The island is nearly equally divided between the establishment and the Nons. As there is a kirk already on the island a site is refused to the non intrusionists, who nevertheless are going to build on the opposite coast.

Lowrie obtained a supply of eggs, potatoes, milk and oatcake and we returned to the ship.

Plate 7 Drawing of Iona village by Colin McVean, a son of the Free Church minister. It appeared in W. Maxwell's *Iona and the Ionians* in 1857. The Carraig Fhada, used as a landing-place, is in the right-hand foreground.

Plate 8 Pigs snooze in the sun at Maol farm. Most people kept pigs again after the potato famine years. (Taken by Mrs. William Crawford, early 1900s.)

NOT A PIG IN IONA

This section comes entirely from one small book written in 1849 by an American, the Rev. J.C. Richmond. This was such a crucial period in the island's history, and his account is so rich in interesting detail, that it deserves to be read at length.

In 1849 the potato blight, which had first struck much of the West Highlands three years earlier, was still rife. The consequences had been disastrous. Almost overnight, the people lost both a staple food and a saleable commodity. Deprived of fodder, the livestock - and even the pigs - were drastically reduced. By a unhappy coincidence, other sources of cash earnings had been declining over the previous decade or so and the island had found itself with little food and little means to buy any extra. Richmond's reference to the use of eggs as currency graphically illustrates this. In response to the crisis, numbers had begun to emigrate - many assisted with passage money to Canada by the Argyll Estate - on a scale which Iona had never known before. Between the Census of 1841 and that of 1851 the population dropped from 496 to 337 and by 1861 it was only 263.

Despite the hardship of the times, however, Richmond's impressions are by no means all negative. He was impressed by the cleanliness of the inn and with the simple but healthy food provided by the landlady. The value placed by the people on Sabbath observance remained strong, despite the temptation to earn money. There is a tribute to the dedication of Allan MacLean, the schoolmaster.

On his arrival, Mr. Richmond received an invitation to tea from the Free Church minister, the Rev. Donald McVean. In the course of the week he clearly spent some time with the family who were then living in the recently built Free Church Manse (now the Columba Hotel). Staying as a guest of the household at that time was the young Henry D. Graham, later to become known for his books *The Antiquities of Iona* and *The Birds of Iona*.

Mr. Richmond found that his name immediately struck a chord on Iona. The visiting clergyman of nearly thirty years before, the Rev. Legh Richmond, left a lasting legacy. He had taken a particular interest in the schoolchildren, organising a grand picnic on the shore for them prior to his departure, and funds he raised were used to buy books. These were among the first to form the island's library collection. A brass plaque, made by local craftsman Alex Ritchie, hangs above the fireplace in the present library building to commemorate this gift.

1849 : Rev. James C. Richmond

About thirty years ago in 1820 the Rev. Legh Richmond visited Iona and, by his successful exertions on behalf of the poor islanders, left a name behind him which will not easily be forgotten. In 1823 the visit was repeated; and when I saw 'the good schoolmaster' Allan Maclean, now in his 88th year, I soon found that the arrival of this benevolent clergyman was *the event* in that long life. ...that subject, of which he is never weary, is his 'friend, the eminent divine'... The name was all sufficient; and the visit being prolonged, the first three sermons that I have preached in Scotland were to many of the old friends of Legh Richmond and delivered in a small stone hut on the consecrated soil of Icolmkill. ...

When the good old schoolmaster came to this island, about 60 years ago, only two persons could read English; and even those, according to the absurd mode of education which long prevailed in the Highlands, could not understand what they read.

...Now there is not a house without someone able to speak, read and understand both languages. Fifteen years ago the good schoolmaster endeavoured to persuade the adults to learn and at length had the satisfaction of seeing some of them assembled in his lowly cabin. A new fear arose - that his candles would not hold out during the long winter evenings. Soon, however, the improvement was so manifest that the people put their little means together for the purchase of tallow; and by these contributions, with the addition of oil obtained from the fish which they had caught - which oil they still burn in a most antique and primitive lamp - the schoolmaster was enabled to light up his cabin and to throw some rays into their minds.

...

I saw several clocks and did not count the number of watches; but I understand there is an individual who dignifies himself with the name of 'merchant' in Bailemor [the village]... Those who have time to examine the manner in which commercial affairs are conducted in Iona might seek out the merchant's abode where they may see an ounce of that new luxury, tea, or the like amount of that Highland necessity of life, tobacco, sold for so many eggs which are laid down in the same manner as half-pence except that being formerly estimated at a farthing each the standard is now raised, and their value is a third of a penny.

The people are excessively poor and like most of the inhabitants of the Hebrides have been reduced by the failure of the potato to such extreme destitution that many of them, especially among the cottars, are now supported by relief from the Central Committee of the charitable fund at Glasgow and would otherwise have perished. The cottars usually have a little garden attached to their miserable stone huts, most of which stand in a row on the shore and are thatched with straw which is kept from being blown away during storms by stones attached to ropes of heather and descending to the eaves. The interior does not differ from the usual Highland hut, being small, smoky and thoroughly uncomfortable..

Some of the people are employed in weaving the plaids, in almost universal use in these Northern regions; and sometimes two of them join their forces and become quite rich by being owners of a boat, with which they can often go out a short distance and catch a few small codfish, flounders and ling; and sometimes large numbers of gurnet, which assists them in sustaining life.

But the failure of the potato has made these poor people still more wretched. I shall hardly be believed if I state the fact that there is now, on account of that failure, not a pig in Iona... But the poor poultry have suffered also, as much as the porkers, from the loss of the potato... As the grass has not failed, the poor people still have their cows; but even these, at the end of the winter, when the small pittance of straw and hay is consumed, miss the root which was once used to sustain them until the grass grew abundantly again. ...the poverty of the people has become so great that, through means furnished by the Duke of Argyll, fifty lately emigrated in one body and not two years ago, one hundred left their homes, those poor cottages which now stand melancholy and deserted.

On my arrival a stone hut, without sign, but of somewhat better appearance than the neighbouring cottages, was pointed out to me as the only house in the place which might, by courtesy, be called an Inn. ...There was a room on each side of the door and a closet, which might be called a small bed-room, in front of it. Three rooms! This was already a great deal, where we had reason to expect only one. In the kitchen the peat upon the 'hearth-stane' sent forth volumes of fragrant smoke that penetrated into and filled the room for the guests, which contained two narrow beds. The floor was of the original soil; but a grate had been set and a good peat fire prevented it from being so damp and cold as it might otherwise have been; for it was a November day in July and summer seems just thinking of coming here.

The landlord and his wife were most respectful, attentive and kind; and it was remarkable, under circumstances to outwardly unfavourable, that everything was scrupulously neat. I enjoyed the primitive style beyond measure;...those who cannot be content with the primordial simplicity of Donald MacPhail are not fit to appreciate Iona... The landlady fetched a few small fish, fresh eggs, oatmeal cakes baked with the girdle, a little tea and milk - the daughter having taken her usual walk of two miles that morning and would go again that evening to the end of the island to milk the cows. With these materials we made a delicious meal.

My friend the Rev. D. McVean has already planted a garden; and the only trees upon the island, with the exception of two or three stunted bushes that would never be called trees anywhere else, were set out by his hand. When I was taken into the garden by the children it was not for the purpose of seeing such a wonder in Iona but for feeding the hoody crow. This bird had been taken on the rocks by Mr. Graham. The children were also tending a young tame gull and one, Colin, showed off his collection of birds' eggs.

[Mr. McVean] has not only instructed his parishioners by his example in the arts of gardening and agriculture but, when there was no doctor residing on the island he and his lady were obliged also to dispense medicines and give advice to the people, having a care of their bodies as well as a cure of souls. ...About two-thirds of the people with their minister left the Establishment together...The kirk was also given up and I officiated in the usual place of worship, a poor dark stone hut without a floor. But...today I saw the roof put upon the neat little church, which will be finished before Winter.

I shall be permitted to mention a circumstance that occurred the other day and which must be considered as remarkable when the extreme poverty of the people is remembered. A Frenchman was here on Sunday June 24th and wishing a boat to convey him to Staffa found it impossible to obtain one on that day. The usual price is six or seven shillings and he actually raised his offers until the bribe of three guineas, or nine times the common hire, became too strong for a couple of the boys. But after they had put off their boat, a relative stood upon the shore and, assisted by the poor fellows' own conscience, persuaded them to return.

When it is recollected that employment at one shilling a day is eagerly sought and obtained without difficulty, and that these poor lads sacrificed *sixty days wages* for a few hours work, on the Lord's Day, I must say that it is an example that deserves to be quoted and remembered. The man's name, who called the boys back, was Neil MacDonald. Not a boat could be obtained at any price in Iona though the foreigner finally succeeded in getting one from the Ross of Mull.

Two years ago there was another example on the occasion of the visit of the Grand Duke Constantine of Russia, who came on the Queen's yacht. The people did not unlock the gates of the ruins for him as it was a Sunday and the brother of the autocrat of all the Russias was obliged to jump over the iron gate at his own proper peril while his suite remained without.

Plate 9 Iona Cottage, to the left, was the inn where the Rev. J. C. Richmond stayed in 1849. Below it, children have a stall set up for their pebbles and shells. (Photo taken mid-1890s)

Plate 10 Girls show visitors from *The Grenadier* souvenirs from shells. (From a postcard by J. Valentine, late 19th century.)

THESE LITTLE MERCHANTS

The Preface of Keddie's informative little guidebook states: 'The profits arising from the sale of this volume will be devoted to educational purposes, under the direction of Rev. Mr. McVean of Iona'. A visitor in 1848 commented on a collection made aboard their steamer towards a Free Church school on the island, an initiative presumably taken by Mr. McVean. Whether the sale of this book was toward the same ends is not known.

As has become obvious in a number of these extracts, the children seldom failed to catch the visitor's attention from the moment he or she landed. Keddie is one of the few to offer an explanation for the selling of pebbles - a throwback to the religious relics of former centuries.

The booklet by G.T. (full name unknown) also aimed to benefit the islanders, and in particular the children, both through its sales and through added publicity for the 'Boat Scheme'. This was a fund to purchase fishing boats, nets and tackle, begun in Skye by Dr. Alexander Fletcher and then extended to Mull and Iona. On the same trip was Thomas Cook, who had been conducting his package tours to the West of Scotland since 1848. He took a great interest in Iona. He was involved in the fishing boat scheme and, later, donated a medicine chest to the school and a bookcase filled with 250 volumes for the island's library collection.

The extract from William Maxwell presents a contrasting view of the children, and a decidedly uncomplimentary one! His entire book, however, is a catalogue of complaint and he represents that school of visitor whose fixed notions prevented them from appreciating differences in culture and lifestyle. He was offended by the cattle roaming in the Cathedral ruins and by the landing-place and the roads; he judged the crofting system old-fashioned and the crofters lazy; he found their traditional beliefs absurd and their custom of swimming horses barbarous. This kind of sweeping condemnation, if it became known, did not go down well with the local people. It may not be a coincidence that a presentation copy of Maxwell's book, found in a collection once owned by an Iona minister, had the author's signature firmly scored out.

Allan MacLean's reign as guide had by now ended. Crofter Angus Lamont had taken over in 1840, to be succeeded in turn by his daughter Mary in 1857 until about 1863. Archibald MacDonald, and later his son John, then acted as boatman and guide.

1850 : William Keddie

The present number of inhabitants of Iona is about 350, forming about 65 families. The population has been greatly diminished, of late years, by emigration. Upwards of thirty families hold crofts in various parts of the island. And the rest is clustered in the village over against the landing place and follow the occupations of tailors, cobblers, carpenters and weavers; many of them are also owners of boats and unite fishing to their other avocations. The people make most of their own clothing... A friend who has witnessed the waulking in Iona informs us that as the work grows warm the song waxes louder and louder... The natives weave a Culdee tartan plaid ... They have an ancient practice also of forming a milk jug, of antique appearance, out of clay found on the island.

There is no corn mill in the island; and the grain is conveyed eight miles, by water, to Bunessan, in Mull to be ground. When the mill is out of gear or the stream fails, which is no unknown occurrence, the islanders resort to the use of the quern or handmill. There are two of these mills in Iona which, in cases of necessity are passed from house to house and are in constant operation, night and day. This labour always devolves upon the females.

Two large boats are in attendance upon the steamer as soon as she casts anchor. The chief boatman is named Archibald MacDonald who, after landing the visitors, accompanies them in the capacity of guide and interpretor. He will be found an intelligent and civil man and the tourist who desires to visit Staffa, or the neighbouring islands, in a small boat, may confide in him as a steady and skilful steersman. He carries the keys of the enclosures, acting as assistant to Mr. Angus Lamont the venerable custodian of the relics...

The moment the stranger sets his foot on shore, he is acccosted by groups of poorly clad, but clean and healthy children, eagerly proffering for sale collections of shells and pebbles neatly arranged on small plates. This is a very old custom, originating in the practice of pilgrims carrying away relics and charms from the island. ...The pebble (serpentine) was esteemed anti-magical, medicinal and a preservative against shipwreck.

1857 : William Maxwell

At the present time there are not more than two hundred inhabitants, old and young, in Iona, and every year the number is decreasing. Emigration thins their ranks, added to which, situations in the low country daily tempt the youth of both sexes to push their fortunes and better their conditions in life. Notwithstanding the paucity of the people, there are two churches on the island, the Established Church of Scotland, and the Free Church, in addition to which, there is a Baptist preacher.

Education is cared for; the parochial school being ably conducted and numerously attended, especially during the winter season when no labour out of doors withdraws the attention of the pupils from their studies. ...Apart from fishing, weaving is the principal occupation of the people, added to that we must not forget two sons of Crispin, a tailor, and a brace of general merchants. Neither must we omit the post-office, the keeper of which, "a ruler in Israel", combines in his own person nearly all the trades in the island, besides being a "man in authority", as cicerone to the ruins during the summer season, the which, unless common report greatly err, is worth all the others put together.

...IONIAN CURIOSITY-SELLERS Without ocular demonstration, it is impossible to conceive the impertinence and pertinacity of the urchins of Iona in their attempts to effect a sale of their trifling curiosities. If an individual notice their selections of pebbles or shells, they all cluster around him, holding up their treasures to his very nose, with such an outcry of discordant voices as would disturb the equanimity of the most apathetic. On no day do they appear more ragged or dirty than on "steam-boat days", with the view we suppose of influencing the tender sensibilities of the charitable. Woe betide that hapless tourist whom they find alone, for they surround him, *nolens volens,* until he opens his purse strings as a quit-offering.

With the exception of the parents of those thus engaged, all living here reprobate their conduct. The clergymen and teacher have no influence over them, as, when the chance of money's in the case, all other things give place; they absent themselves from school in spite of all remonstrances. Unlike bashful Highland children in general, for barefacedness and impudence the youngsters of Iona might stand side by side with Glasgow juvenile criminals.

1858 : G.T.

The object of bringing before the public this little book is three-fold. To extend the knowledge of and secure funds to the 'Boat Scheme' originated by the late Dr. Fletcher. To supply a felt want by the children in Iona in giving these little merchants a something to sell besides the shells and pebbles of the island which, according to the ancient custom, they meet the tourists with. And if possible also, to secure by its sale a sum sufficient for the purchase of a fishing boat - which will support three families

- to receive a name in remembrance more particularly of Dr. Fletcher as 'The Childrens Fund'.

...

The children gather the finer and brighter coloured sorts of seaweed and then arrange it upon paper. From time to time some of these beautiful specimens have been specially prepared by grateful little fingers and forwarded through the post to me... During the stay of the steamer the grounds surrounding the now ruined Nunnery serve for the time being the purpose of, shall I call it, the Iona Bazaar. Each little child - not ragged though very poor - has her own appointed stall at which the tourists can make their purchases.

[The party had come from Oban on the paddle steamer the *Pioneer*.] On entering the Sound of Iona, a salute from the ship's gun announced our arrival, the *Legh Richmond* and *Thomas Cook* fishing boats each hoisting their respective flags, loudly cheering the arrival of their newly built companion, the *Duke of Argyle* , brought in tow of the steamer from Oban.

After a sermon in the Cathedral... on our return to the steamer we were kindly presented with more than one glass of the sweetest milk ever drank, with oatcake and scones and in one lowly cottage some tea carried by a friend was quickly prepared with true Highland hospitality, with the addition of boiled flounder, oatcake and butter - a kindly look and friendly grasp of the hand being all the thanks needed or understood.

The crews of the respective fishing boats looked clean, comfortable and highly delighted and that of the *Thomas Cook* not a little proud to convey their friend under his own flag back to the *Pioneer*.

[In Mr. Cook's own words]... In our visit today, which numbers my fortieth to Iona, I could not help being struck with the spirit of earnestness and hope... ten months ago it was a difficult matter to find three men possessed of sufficient energy to make a venture with the first boat.. they now have paid off in good part the instalments on their boats... one boatman told me his boat had taken 26 tons of fish.

Plate 11 Locals and visitors going into the Post Office on the village street, run there by the MacDonald family from 1851 until 1896.

QUITE A NINETEENTH CENTURY PLACE

In 1889 John MacCormick, a native of the Ross of Mull and co-founder of The Iona Press, wrote in an article for the *Oban Times* that in Iona 'Civilisation has firmly established itself...and many strangers visiting the island during the summer months are surprised to find it quite a nineteenth century place'. He was referring particularly to the disappearance of customs rooted in superstitious belief, such as that of 'am brochan mòr'. In this ceremony, on the Thursday before Easter, oatmeal was cast into the sea as an offering to the sea-god in order to ensure a good supply of wrack to fertilise the fields for the next year's crop.

There were other changes too by the last quarter of the century and the final extracts reflect some of them. Two hotels now catered for visitors: the Columba Hotel, converted from the first Free Church manse in 1868; and the Argyll Hotel in the village street, for some years a shop and then built up to provide inn accommodation in 1867. A number of other two-storied, slated houses appeared and although many cottages were still thatched, most had gable-ends with chimneys and burned coal, replacing the peat-fired central hearth of former years. The island was by no means isolated. Several local people contributed regular items to newspapers which were, in turn, eagerly read. A policeman was now based on the Ross of Mull, although - in 1870 at least - it did not sound as if his presence was very intrusive in Iona! There was a post office on the island and a steamer link direct to the Clyde, for cargo, livestock and passage.

The good quality of the crops, livestock and dairy produce caught the eye of these late 19th century visitors as they had those of one and two hundred years before. The crisis of the late 1840s had been weathered and the land remained the basis of the island's economy.

The first contributor, John Gillespie, is the only visitor I have come across to write about the wreck of the *Guy Mannering*. The memorial to the sailors who drowned was not erected in the Rèilig Orain until 1882, as a result of a visit by the U.S. Consul in Glasgow, Mr. Bret Harte. The ship met its end on a rock off the Machair shore (ever since named Brown's Rock after the Captain) in the late afternoon of 31 December 1865. Royal Humane Society medals and testimonials were awarded to seven islanders for their heroic efforts to rescue nineteen of the crew.

The preface to the Pennell's book is dated 1888 but it was based on a series of articles published some years earlier and the conversation with the ferryman indicates that their visit to Mull and Iona nearly coincided with that of the Royal Commission of inquiry into crofters' conditions in 1883. Thus, questions of land, rents and relations with landlords were much to the fore. The Pennells, unusually, had undertaken their tours on foot and many of their observations were far from complimentary to either countryside or inhabitants in the Highlands. Their articles had been condemned as impertinent, a charge stoutly refuted by the writers who claimed that they had simply recorded actual conditions as they saw them. Iona, by contrast, they found well-cultivated and hospitable.

Malcolm Ferguson's whole book is highly recommended for the wealth of detail he includes about the housing, farming, trades and customs of the island. He was an enthusiastic travel writer with an inquiring mind and an observant eye. And, very importantly, he was keen to use local knowledge as much as possible. On arriving in Iona he was amused to find a namesake to act as guide and informant during his stay - crofter Malcolm Ferguson, known locally as Calum Bàn. There is room here to give only a flavour of Ferguson's colourful style. But the obvious pleasure he derived from his visit will strike a chord with many who have returned again and again to Iona and it seems appropriate, therefore, to allow the closing words of his book to bring this collection to an end.

1870 : John Gillespie

It must have been a sorry New Year for Captain Brown of the American ship the *Guy Mannering* when he laid the poor fellows one by one in their graves in the lone churchyard of Iona, far from their homes and kindred. The Captain and 18 of the sailors were saved. The crew numbered 34. The Captain, noble fellow! was the last the leave his ship and was taken out of the sea apparently dead... The ship (2200 tons) was cotton laden...

...The innkeeper above referred to is a gentleman well known in Greenock. He was for many years Captain of the steamer Islesman. He now farms a portion of land under the Duke of Argyll in Iona. A house formerly occupied by the Rev. Mr. McVean was converted into the St. Columba Hotel and let as such by the Duke of Argyll to Captain Ritchie with the proviso that no whisky or ardent spirits were to be sold therein - indeed no stimulants except wine, porter or ale; and that condition I believe has been faithfully kept.

[The writer crossed briefly to Fionnphort and while there the policeman borrowed his boat to go to Iona and back. The aim of his brief visits was so that the minister sign a paper confirming that he (the policeman) had duly appeared in Iona at the end of each month. Departure was on the *Dunvegan Castle*, which arrived unexpectedly at 3 am on Sunday, sounding its whistle.]

While on board a matter came under my observation and I allude to it as showing deep religious feeling of the Ionians. The steamer was laden with cattle, sheep and pigs. For connoisseurs (owing to pigs being fed in a very cleanly way in the Hebrides) to obtain a pig reared there is reckoned a matter of some importance. A passenger asked an islander if he would sell a pig he had on board and the reply was :'On the Sabbath day not for the whole world would I sell that pig!'

1876 : Constance F. G. Cumming

A colony of jackdaws finds a shelter in the crannies of the great Cathedral tower. The islanders have devious superstitions about these birds which they will on no account molest. They maintain that since the days of St. Columba they have claimed a home in his monastery and that their numbers have never either increased or decreased but that they are uncanny birds and know many things.

Pit an druidh, the cairn that marks the burial place of St.Columba's predecessors. An old man who had the English, in addition to his Gaelic mother tongue, told me that he had seen this grave opened..and a great heap of human bones. ...near this place stands the only cottage still on the isle with the old fashioned fireplace hollowed in the centre of the earthen floor and with no chimney except a hole in the middle of the roof. It inmates gave me a cordial welcome, my old friend who 'had the English' being the gude-man of the house, so he heaped on fresh peats and invited me to sit awhile and chat beside the cheery blaze.

...

There is charm even in the name of the little inn. Fancy being welcomed to St.Columba's Arms! To such as can appreciate the excellence and abundance of dairy produce, the bowls of creamy milk and snowy curds are an attraction in themselves. Such fresh floury scones too, baked by the most motherly of highland landladies!

1883 : Elizabeth and Joseph Pennell

All this part of the Ross of Mull as far as we could see belonged to the Duke of Argyll, our ferryman said. There had been trouble here as in Tiree and the Commission was coming in a week. We had only his house and his boat. 5/6 he paid; it was not much but it was about the land there was trouble and he had no land.

...

Iona is the showplace by which we fancied the Duke of Argyll must hope to answer the question, once in a great while asked, about misery, terrorism, extortion, rent in the Hebrides. Strangers come to the islands only to fish or to shoot. It is the exception when, as at Iona, there are sights to be seen. They have time to give only a glance to the islander and his home. In Iona this home seems decent enough; if you stop to ask an islander what he thinks, however, I doubt if it will be praise alone you will hear of his model landlord. Above the stony beach, where bays lie among the rocks, is the village street lined with white cottages; and beyond, fields of tall grain and good pasture slope upwards to the foot of the low green hills... Many of the cottages are new, others are whitewashed into comparative cheerfulness.

...

It is the fashion among writers of guide and other books about Iona to call it a desolate, lonely little isle. That it is little I admit; but you must go to the other side of the Sound for loneliness and desolation. In proportion to its size it seemed to us the most cultivated island of the Hebrides. ...Even where it is, it has crowds of visitors. The writer who on one page tells us of its loneliness, on the next mourns its daily desecration when tourists eat sandwiches among the ruins.

...

People who have never heard of crofters and their troubles can tell you all about St.Columba and his miracles. In Iona he interested us chiefly because all that is left of his and his followers' work gives the lie to modern landlords. Land in the Hebrides, they say, is all fit for deer and grouse. St.Columba showed that it could be made fit for man as well. The landlady of St. Columba's Inn is true to the traditions of the island. She is as unwilling to turn the stranger from her door as were the abbots of St. Columba's monastery. In her own way she performs miracles and finds room for everyone who comes. ...It was at the late supper that we enjoyed the 'dairy produce' of which Miss Gordon Cumming writes with rapture. It was a simple meal such as one might have shared with St.Columba himself. The breakfasts and dinners, I should add, were less saintly and therefore more substantial.

Plate 12 Visitors pose in front of the three thatched cottages at the
head of Iona jetty, about 1905. Lachlan Maclean's wife and
daughters are at the door of the centre cottage; their family ran a
shop there from the 1830s to the 1960s.

Plate 13 Stirks on Fionnphort jetty after being transported from Iona in the ferry boat. (Photo by Mrs. William Crawford, early 1900s.)

Plate 14 Horse led ashore at Iona after being swum from Fionnphort. (Photo taken by visitor Miss McFee in August 1909.)

Plate 15 Cnoc Cùl Phàil, the house where crofter Malcolm Ferguson lived. (Photographer and date unknown, probably 1930s.)

Plate 16 Johnnie Campbell, Lagandòrain, churning butter, probably in the 1930s. Iona's abundant dairy food was praised by many visitors.

1891 : William Winter

Iona...contains about two thousand acres of land, of which about a quarter is under cultivation - for oats, hay, vegetables and flowers. Three-quarters of it are devoted to pasture. There are within its limits of cattle, horses, sheep and other animals about a thousand. The collie dog and the household cat are frequently encountered and you will not stroll far upon the moors without meeting the dark and stately Highland bull.

I counted about fifty dwellings... All the houses are made of stone and some of them have a roof of thatch which is held in its place by clamps, superincumbent timbers and heavy weights of stone or iron. The crofters, all of whom are prosperous, live in little stone cottages, rarely more than one storey high. The village consists of a single street, with those humble huts ranged upon one side of it, their doors and windows facing eastwards toward the Sound. The post office is also a shop and there are two or three shops beside. Three times a week a little steamboat, sailing out of Bunessan - a town of Mull...- calls at Iona if she can and takes away a mail and leaves one, touching by means of a skiff at St.Ronan's Bay.

The inhabitants are generally religious and are orderly, courteous and gentle. No doctor dwells in the place and no resident of it is ever sick. Death may come by drowning or by other accident but as a rule the people live until they are worn out, and so expire, naturally, from extreme age. The Gaelic language is still spoken here. The minister, preaching on alternate Sundays at Iona and at Bunessan, speaks in English first and then repeats his discourse in Gaelic, or he reverses that order.

The school is largely followed - the present attendance being nearly seventy pupils - and in the schoolhouse I found a library of nearly 500 books. ...No newspaper is published at Iona but there is a little printing office near the St. Columba hotel and from that germ may be expected, one day or another, such practical growth of enterprise and of civilising thought as follows in the track of a wisely ordered press.   ·

1893 : Malcolm Ferguson

Here, as at Staffa, there was a large red-painted boat with room for fifty or sixty people, with a crew of four stout, active-looking rowers lying waiting to take the passengers ashore. ...while my fellow passengers were getting into the landing boats I had a splendid bird's eye view of Ballimore - ie Big Town... The picturesque little Highland village consists of twenty dwellings extending along the shore on either side of the landing-place. A number of the old, thatched, primitive-looking houses have recently been rebuilt with stone and lime and slated, presenting very neat, tidy, two-storied, self-contained cottages.

...

Last summer being phenomenally dry and fine, every letting house and odd room in the place were crammed with visitors, who had found their way to Iona to spend their summer holidays. ...As the passengers from the steamer walked up along the uneven rocky jetty towards the open space or square in front of the houses, there was an eager crowd of natives, mingled with their temporary lodgers and visitors, surveying with evident keen interest and curiosity the new arrivals by the *Grenadier* , not a few of whom, by their unique rig-out, had a decidedly foreign look about them....

...

A large portion of the arable land consists of a rich gravelly soil and produces excellent crops of various sorts, considering its being so continually under crop. I was much surprised after landing to see as heavy and luxuriant crops on some fields as I had seen last season in any part of Scotland. The principal crops raised are bere, rye, oats, potatoes and ryegrass hay. Not a boll of grain has been either imported or exported for the last forty years. In summer the pastures are very rich and luxuriant, and suitable for dairy farming and for rearing cattle and sheep. The chief commodities exported from the island are Highland cattle, sheep, pigs and eggs.

A special drawback with the Iona farmers and crofters is the great difficulty experienced in removing cattle and horses when being sent to markets for sale. A cattle market is held three times a year at Bunessan in Mull, some eight or nine miles from Iona, with the Sound to cross. Most of the cattle dealers are local farmers. A horse market is held once a year at Salen, Mull, a distance of 30 miles from Iona. When ferrying cattle across the Sound on their way to markets to be sold a boat is brought to the beach but kept afloat. Two strong active men stand up to their middle in the water; the one grasps the animal by the forelegs, the other by the hindlegs and back to back pull with their hands, and give a sudden shove with their shoulders and the animal is whummelled heels over head into the boat, landing with a dull-sounding thud in the bottom of the wherry. Other men are standing in the boat ready to tie its four legs firmly together with strong ropes and it is then stowed in the bottom of the craft.

Brackens and other soft substances are spread on the floor of the boat as a comfortable bedding... ...but when a big, bellowing, fierce-looking Highland bull...has to be taken across the operation is 'nae joke'. To see a four-year old Highland bull - then in his prime - lashing itself with its tail, tearing up the sward with its powerful, hardy fore-hoofs...he presents a picture of infuriated rage which once seen is not easily forgotten. Instead of tumbling the bulls into a ferry-boat...a stout rope is tied round about the roots of the bull's horns, it is then dragged by sheer force into the sea and towed across the Sound after a boat... Horses when being sent off to market to be sold are treated the same as the bulls. Such work, however, requires a great deal of caution and experience, as it is always accompanied with a considerable amount of risk and danger.

...

After spending a most enjoyable week's holiday on the island, being favoured with splendid, clear, bright weather, I left one afternoon at three p.m. by the *Grenadier* on her homeward run round the south coast of Mull - the sea as smooth as a mill pond - and after three hours' pleasant sail landed at Oban at six p.m.

Having for long had a strong desire to see Iona, I am thankful that I have been privileged to enjoy such a pleasant visit to the sacred Island, from which for so many generations there shone the light of religion and civilisation when the rest of the country was enveloped in heathen darkness.

CIRCULAR TOURS.

Oban to Staffa and Iona.

By Steamer "GRENADIER" daily at 8 a.m., returning in the evening. Cabin Return Fare, 15s., includes Guides and Boatmen.

✳ ✳ ✳

OBAN to STAFFA and IONA and Back.

Daily from 31st May till 30th September. For fares see page 17.

GOING NORTH.		Mo. Wed. and Fri.	GOING SOUTH.		Tu. Thur. and Sat.
Oban	Steamer lea.	8 0a	Oban	Steamer lea.	8 0a
Craignure ..	,,	8 45	Carsaig	,,	9 15
Lochaline	,,	9 5	Iona	arr.	10 30
Salen	,,	9 30	do., ...	dep.	12 0
Tobermory	,,	10 15	Staffa	arr.	12 30p
Staffa	arr.	11 45	do., ...	dep.	1 45
do., ...	dep.	1 15p	Tobermory	,,	3 0
Iona	arr.	1 45	Salen	,,	3 30
do., ...	dep.	3 15	Lochaline	,,	4 0
Carsaig	,,	4 15	Craignure	,,	4 30
Oban	,,	5 30	Oban	,,	5 30
Train for Glasgow & the South lea.		—	Train for Glasgow & the South lea.		—

✳ ✳ ✳

TARIFF OF CHARGES IN DINING SALOONS.

	Cabin.	Fore Cabin.		Cabin.	Fore Cabin.
Breakfast,	2/-	1/6	Dinner,	3/-	2/-
Luncheon,	2/-		Tea (with Meat),	2/-	1/6

Plain Tea (in Cabin), ... 1/-.

Dinner 6d. less on Glasgow & Ardrishaig and Crinan & Oban Steamers.

Cup of Tea or Coffee with Biscuit, - 6d.	Whisky, Rum, and Gin, - per Glass. 6d.
Beer, Porter, Aerated Waters, per Bot. 6d.	Brandy, - - - - per Glass. 9d.

CIGARS, CIGARETTES, CUT TOBACCOES, &c.

Wines of every description and of the best vintages kept on board.
See Special Wine List.

From a David MacBrayne's guidebook of 1897.

BIBLIOGRAPHY

ANONYMOUS, 'Tour of my Native Country particularly of the Highlands', (manuscript journal, Aberdeen University Library 1023)

BAILEY, James, 'Journey in Scotland with sketches of some picturesque ruins in that interesting country', (manuscript journal written 1787, NLS.3295)

BOSWELL, James, *Journal of a Tour to the Hebrides,* (1st edition, London 1785)

BOWMAN, J.E., *The Highlands and Islands. A Nineteenth Century Tour,* (Gloucester 1986)

BOYLE, G.F., 'Journal of a Voyage to Staffa and Iona in the Amina yacht of 19 tons', (manuscript dated June 1844, St.Andrews University library, 36365)

BUTE, John 1st Marquess of, 'Journal of the Tour round the Western Islands of Scotland 1788', (manuscript journal, NLS.9587)

CARR, Sir John, *Caledonian Sketches or a Tour through Scotland in 1807,* (London 1809)

CARRUTHERS, Robert, *The Highland Notebook or Sketches and Anecdotes,* (Edinburgh 1843)

CUMMING, Constance F.G., *From the Hebrides to the Himalayas,* 2 volumes, (1st edition, London 1876)

DOUGLAS, George, 'Tour in the Hebrides AD 1800', (manuscript journal, NLS.213)

DUCOS, Bernard, *Itineraire et Souvenirs d'Angleterre et d'Ecosse 1814-1826,* 4 volumes, (Paris 1834)

FERGUSON, Malcolm, *A Visit to Staffa and Iona,* (Dundee & Edinburgh 1894)

GARNETT, Thomas, *Observations on a Tour through the Highlands and part of the Western Isles of Scotland,* 2 volumes, (London 1810)

GILLESPIE, John, *Iona. Churchyard and Cathedral. Staffa,* (Greenock Telegraph 1871)

HEAD, Sir George, *A Home Tour through various parts of the United Kingdom,* (London 1837)

JOHNSON, James (pseudonym Frederick Fag), *Recess in the Highlands and Lowlands*, (London 1834)

KEDDIE, William, *Staffa and Iona Described and Illustrated*, (Glasgow, Edinburgh & London 1850)

LUMSDEN & Son's *Steam-Boat Companion*, (1st edition Glasgow 1820, 2nd edition 1825, 3rd edition 1831)

MACCULLOCH, Dr. John, *The Highlands and Western Isles of Scotland containing descriptions of their scenery and antiquity*, (London 1824). Based on letters to Sir Walter Scott from annual journeys made between 1811 and 1821. Internal evidence indicates the Iona visit to be before 1819.

MACFARLANE, Walter, *MacFarlane's Geographical Collections, Vol.II*, (Scottish History Society, Edinburgh, Vol.LII, 1907).

MARTIN, Martin, *A Description of the Western Islands of Scotland*, (1st edition, London 1703)

MAXWELL, William, *Iona and the Ionians*, (Glasgow 1857)

MONRO, Sir Donald, Dean of the Isles, *A Description of the Western Isles of Scotland called Hybrides*, (1st edition Edinburgh 1774).

MURRAY, The Hon. Mrs. Sarah of Kensington, *A Companion and Useful Guide to the Beauties in the West Highlands of Scotland and in the Hebrides, Vol.II*, (1st edition, London 1803)

NECKER DE SAUSSURE, L.A., *A Voyage to the Hebrides*, (London 1822)

PENNANT, Thomas, *A Tour in Scotland and Voyage to the Hebrides 1772*, (London 1776)

PENNELL, Joseph and Elizabeth, *Our Journey to the Hebrides*, (London 1890)

POCOCKE, Bishop, *Pococke's Tours in Scotland*, edited by D. W. Kemp, (Scottish History Society, Volume 1, Edinburgh 1887).

RICHMOND, Rev. James C., *A Visit to Iona: by an American Clergyman*, (Glasgow 1849)

SACHEVERELL, Dr. W., Governor of Man, *An Account of the Isle of Man...with a voyage to I-Columb-Kill*, (London 1701).

G.T. (full name not known), *Three Days in the Highlands with the late Reverend A. Fletcher in 1858 with especial reference to Staffa and Iona*, (London 1861)

TEIGNMOUTH, Lord, *Sketches of the Coasts and Islands of Scotland and of the Isle of Man,* 2 volumes, (London 1836)

TOWNSHEND, Chauncy H., *A Descriptive Tour in Scotland,* (Brussels 1840; London 1846)

WALKER, Rev. Dr. John, 'A Natural History of the Island of Icolumbkil' (manuscript La III.575, Edinburgh University Library). See also Walker, *An Economical History of the Hebrides and Highlands of Scotland,* 2 volumes, (Edinburgh 1808); and Walker, *Report on the Hebrides of 1764 and 1771,* edited by M. M. McKay, (Edinburgh 1980).

WILSON, James, *A Voyage round the Coasts of Scotland,* (Edinburgh 1842)

WINTER, William, *Old Shrines and Ivy,* (Edinburgh 1892)

A' Chrìoch